The Good Things

Does for Us, to Us, and Through Us

MICHAEL KOTCH

ISBN 978-1-64349-643-6 (paperback)
ISBN 978-1-64349-644-3 (digital)

Christian Faith Publishing, Inc.
832 Park Avenue
Meadville, PA 16335
www.christianfaithpublishing.com

Printed in the United States of America

Contents

Introduction

I have been a licensed psychologist in the state of Pennsylvania since 2005, with experience at a variety of counseling agencies dating back to 1989. Since 2006, I have been working at a Christian counseling outpatient private practice in Southeast Pennsylvania. The sign hanging up in front of my agency says "Christ-based counseling" under the name of the office. It is a place where the counselors love the God of Christianity and employ Bible-based principles into the counseling *if the client wants it*. The majority of clients come to my practice because they are Christian, and they want counselors that have strong Christian values. They also want biblical guidance infused into their counseling, where applicable.

Some of my clients are not Christian and therefore do not want Christian counseling. Some are Christian, but they don't want Christianity mixed in with their therapy. That's fine, since I am trained as a "regular" psychologist. I got all of my degrees in counseling and psychology from public, secular universities. I get excited, however, when a client tells me that they want biblical Christianity infused into their counseling. That is usually the reason these particular clients selected my office for therapy. I find that clients who have a strong faith in God, and are well-read in the Bible, do better in counseling in general. No matter what the presenting problem is, they turn to God for help and support. I can see the hand of the Holy Spirit carrying the person through his or her problem when they lean on him. They are also able to utilize a wealth of information about how God wants them to handle things in their life from their deep knowledge of the Bible. Clients who are not Christian, or who have rarely read the Bible, do not have the above-stated benefits to use in dealing with their problems.

Among the Christian clients that do want biblical Christianity infused into their counseling, there is a clear dividing line among them. There are those that are well versed in the Bible and incorporate this into their lives, and there are those who are not. Those that know their Bible well and use what it says in their lives have such a full toolbox of abilities and strategies to cope with problems, and it is wonderful for me to witness. With all other things being equal, these people usually make the best progress on issues. I feel very sympathetic for the Christians who come to see me for help but do not read their Bible. There are so many tools/weapons in the Bible at their disposal to handle the difficulties in their lives that they are completely unaware of. Additionally, they really do not know who God is and who they are in relationship to him. They have no idea that when they accept and follow Christ, they are now his children living on earth. The Holy Spirit is alive and now lives inside of them. They have access to God, who is their Father; Jesus, who is their brother; and the Holy Spirit, who is their guide and comforter. They do not really know what God wants them to do in their lives and how he wants them to interact with others. They do not clearly understand that they are eternal beings, who are just living a moment in the first part of their lives here, and the rest will be in heaven into eternity. They do not understand what God's will is for them. And that he wants them to follow his will while on earth, because he has family business work for them do to that is actually monumentally important in the lives of others. They are unaware of so much. And so much of it is *good*. I have had multiple clients tell me, "I love God, but I am *afraid to read the Bible* because it is all about him punishing me whenever I make any mistake." *No, no, no!*

I initially wrote this book as a handout that I gave to my Christian counseling clients, my fifth grade religious instruction class at my church in which I am the teacher, and to all of my family and friends who wished to read it. One of my main goals in life is to get others to read the Bible and implement what God says in their daily lives. Christians who do not read the Bible have no idea how profoundly this will benefit their lives. This book, along with others that I have written for my clients, students, family, and friends, is intended to give them a glimpse into the wonders in the Bible that are meant for them. Hopefully after reading this book, the readers will be inspired to read the actual Bible more on their own.

I went through the New Testament meticulously and collected all the Bible verses I could find which revealed the *good things* God does for those who love and follow him. It is meant to get people to know the Bible better and incorporate it into their lives. It also shows just how good God is to those that love him and the *amazing* things he has in store for those that accept and follow Jesus. I titled it *The Good Things Jesus Does for Us, to Us, and Through Us* because I discovered that there are different kinds of good things that Jesus does for those who choose to love and follow him. Jesus does things *for* us. For example, he saved us by taking our sins on him and getting punished in our place. This made us sinless before God and allowed us to go to heaven when we die. Additionally, Jesus answers our prayers; gives us strength, peace, and wisdom; protects us; etc.

Jesus also does things *to* the people who choose to follow him. God begins to change that person for the better. When a person asks Jesus to be his or her savior and chooses to follow him, and means it, at that moment God takes away that person's sin, and their once sin-ridden dead soul is born alive. That is where the term "born again" comes from. God the Holy Spirit then enters the person and lives in him. The more the person wants God in him or her to take over and guide his or her life, that is what happens. If you strive to serve God and have God guide and direct your life, that is what you get. As you progressively read God's word in the Bible, start living out what the Bible says in your life and pray; the Holy Spirit continually molds you into becoming more and more like Jesus while you are on earth.

The things Jesus does *to* his followers while they are on earth, such as molding us into the image of him, are profound. However, it *does not compare* to what he does *to* his followers when they die. They are transformed into something wonderful. The Bible is clear that what we are now is nothing like what we will become when we reach

7

heaven. Our being is completely transformed into something glorious that the Bible states is equivalent to, yet somehow different from, angels. When we get to heaven, we will be adopted children of God the Father and actual brothers and sisters to Jesus Christ. The Bible says that while we are on earth as followers of Jesus, we are heirs to his kingdom. When we get to heaven, we will receive our inheritance as members of God's family, and our inheritance is the kingdom of heaven. We will live in God's own house. Jesus prepared rooms for us in his house personally. The Bible says that we will be part of Jesus's body and he will be part of ours. We will be joined together as a husband and wife are joined together. And somehow, we will cooperate with God in judging angels and judging the world. Wow.

Finally, there are things God will do *through* people who follow him. As stated earlier, when we follow him, God starts molding us into the image of Christ while we are on earth. Applying the familiar saying in our daily lives "What would Jesus do?" or "What does God say in the Bible and through prayer to do?" is the point. The amount we read God's word, the Bible, and do what it says in our lives, and have a desire to love and follow God along with daily prayer, determines how much we are molded into his image. The Bible is our Father's personal diary to his children, revealing to us who he is and who we are to him. Additionally, it is his instruction book on how he wants us to live. The more we read it and live how it says to, the more the Holy Spirit molds us into Jesus's image on earth. And the more he can use us as his personal ambassadors here. God does a lot of his work on earth through his people. He will use us more and more on earth to impact others. To love them, help them, tell them about Jesus so they too can be saved, and be an instrument in their Christian development on earth. The moment we accepted Jesus as our savior and became saved, he could have taken us straight up to heaven, as in a rapture. But he didn't. He wants us here. He is our Father, we are his children, and he has work for us to do in the family business, helping his other children on earth in a variety of ways. When these people become saved, they will be our brothers and sisters, all of us together in God's big, loving family, when we reach heaven. God works in partnership through us here on earth, to help our future brothers and with whatever they need now.

This book is comprised of Bible verses that I found in the New Testament on these topics, the good things God does for his followers. They are just what *I found*. There are likely more in there that I didn't see. Additionally, God makes numerous statements in the Old Testament about the good things he will do for the people that love him and follow his word. That may be a future book I will write. Even better, open up the Bible and see all of the good promises God made to his children for yourself. The Bible that I used as a reference for this book is the English Standard Version (ESV) published by Crossway. Well, let's get started.

CHAPTER 1

What Is the Bible, and Why Should We Read It?

T he Bible is God's personal messages to mankind. It is his diary to his children. The Bible fully introduces and explains God to us so we can get to know our Father personally. It is also his instructions to us, informing us on the best way to live our lives and the things he wants his children to do in their lives. God spoke through the human writers who wrote the Bible as they were writing it. Although it was human hands that actually wrote the words in the Bible, it was God who spoke through the writers and completely directed them what to write. That appears to be how God usually chooses to accomplish things on earth. He works in cooperation with people on earth who love and follow him, and he partners jointly with them to accomplish his purposes here. That is one reason why it is so important to read *all* of the Bible: it is difficult to carry out God's instructions if you have no idea what they are, because you never took the time to read his instruction manual to us. The more you both know and *do* what it says in the Bible, the more miraculous things God does in your life. Here are Bible verses that I found in which God states that his word (the Bible) comes from *him* and not the product of human origin:

But as for you, continue in what you have learned and have firmly believed, knowing from whom you learned it and how from childhood you have been acquainted with the sacred writings, which are able to make you wise for salvation through faith in Christ Jesus. *All scripture is breathed out by God* and profitable for teaching, for reproof, for correction, and for training in righteousness, that the man of God may be competent, equipped for every good work. (2 Timothy 3:14–17)

You received the word of God, which you heard from us, you accepted it not as the word of men but what it really is, the word of God, which is at work in you believers. (1 Thessalonians 2:13)

If this book is written to those who love and follow Jesus, who exactly are these people? Well, hopefully it is you. And it easily can be, if you choose. We were all fallen sinners, but we can be saved from this if we choose to. Mankind right from the start sinned, beginning with the first people God created, Adam and Eve. When we sin, we are saying to God, "I don't want to follow you; I want to do what *I want to do, even if it is against what you want.*" God allows us to do this through free will. The whole human race sins, those that follow God and those that do not. Those that follow God honestly have the Holy Spirit in them, guiding them to avoid sin. But we all still mess up and sin from time to time. The good news is that for those that follow Jesus, these sins are forgiven. For those that do not follow Jesus, they don't have the Holy Spirit living inside of them to guide them, and they do not have the wisdom of the Bible to follow in their lives. This may be why unsaved people often do not see God's presence in their lives much.

We have all sinned, and sin is not allowed in heaven. Unless this issue is taken care of, this means that none of us would be allowed to enter into heaven when we die. That is why Jesus came to save us. He took everyone's sin off of us, put it on him, and was punished in our place. To get this benefit of what he did for us, we have to accept it and choose to follow him as our God. Then we are completely sinless in God's eyes. The Holy Spirit comes into us and helps us while we are on earth, and we can then enter heaven when we die because we are now sinless. So who can be saved? God, in his own words, says he desires that *everyone* be saved. We have to choose to do so, however. This is what God says about it:

> Jesus said "I am the bread of life; *whoever comes to me shall not hunger, and whoever believes in me shall never thirst.* All that the Father gives me will come to me, and *whoever comes to me I will never cast out.* For I have come down from heaven, not to do my own will but the will of him who sent me. And this is the will of him who sent me, that I should lose nothing of all that he has given me, but raise it up on the last day. For this is the will of my Father, that everyone who looks on the Son and believes in him should have eternal life, and I will raise him up on the last day." (John 6:35–40)

> *God our Savior desires all people to be saved and to come to the knowledge of the truth.* (1 Timothy 2:3–4)

> Jesus said "For God so loved the world, that he gave his only Son, that *whoever believes in him should not perish but have eternal life.* For God did not send his Son into the world to condemn the world, but in order that the world might be saved through him. Whoever believes in him is not condemned, but whoever does not believe is condemned already, because he has not believed in the name of the only Son of God." (John 3:16–21)

If a person wants to be saved by Jesus (and everyone should want this), how does he or she make it happen? The Apostle Paul explains in the Book of Romans how a person can be saved by Jesus. All you have to do is believe Jesus is God, call on him to save you, and *mean it*:

> If you confess with your mouth that Jesus is Lord and believe in your heart that God raised him from the dead, you will be saved. For with the heart one believes and is justified, and with the mouth one confesses and is saved. For the Scripture says, "Everyone who believes in him will not be put to shame." For there is no distinction between Jew and Greek; for the same Lord is Lord of all, bestowing riches on all who call on him. *For everyone who calls on the name of the Lord will be saved.* (Romans 10:9–13)

God extends his offer for us to be saved to *everyone*, even those who are prevented from hearing the Gospel while on earth. For example, in some countries, such as North Korea, it is illegal to preach about Jesus. Therefore, many people never are told about him. They would have asked him to be their savior, but they never heard about him. God is a completely fair God, and he wants everyone to have the opportunity to be saved. God says in the Bible that for those who never had the chance to hear about Jesus while they were alive, the gospel will be preached to them after death, so everyone will get an opportunity to choose or reject Jesus. This is what God says about it:

> For this is why the gospel was preached to even those who are dead, that though judged in the flesh the way people are, they might live in the spirit the way God does. (1 Peter 4:6)

THE GOOD THINGS JESUS DOES FOR US, TO US, AND THROUGH US

We are fortunate. We live in countries in which we hear about Jesus while we are alive. We can therefore start enjoying the promises he makes to those that follow him while we are still here on earth.

Therefore, one of the *very good* things Jesus does for those that love and follow him is he will save anyone from their sins if they ask him to and then follow him as their God and savior.

CHAPTER 2

God Says the Way to Love Him Is to Do What He Says to Do

Once we become saved, one of the main benefits of this is our sins are forgiven, so we can enter heaven when we die. That is not the only good thing that can happen. The rest of this book explains all of the good things God will do for people who love and follow Jesus. Not just get saved by him and then do nothing for or with God for the rest of your life and have no communication with him. These following promises are for people who, after asking Jesus to be their Lord and savior, then love and follow him in their daily lives. What does it mean to love and follow God? God clearly explains it in the Bible. To love and follow God is to learn what he tells us, and do what he says in our daily lives. Even simpler: read the Bible and do what it says in our lives. And pray with him daily. The Bible is God's complete message to us. It explains who he is, who we are, and what he wants us to do. How are we supposed to know what God wants us to do in our lives if we refuse to read the message he sent us about it? In God's own words, the way for us to love him is to learn what he commands us to do and then do it. Read the Bible, and try to live it out in your life. It's not hard at all. In fact, it is enjoyable and very rewarding. *This is how God says we can love him:*

Jesus said "Whoever has my commandments and keeps them, he it is who loves me.
And he who loves me will be loved by my Father,
and I will love him and manifest myself to him."
(John 14:21)

Jesus said "If you love me, you will keep
my commandments. And I will ask the Father,
and he will give you another Helper, to be with
you forever, even the Spirit of truth, whom the
world cannot receive, because it neither sees him
or knows him. You know him, for he dwells with
you and will be in you." (John 14:15–17)

Jesus said "If anyone loves me, he will keep
my word, and my Father will love him, and we
will come to him and make our home with him."
(John 14:23)

Whatever we ask we receive from God,
because we keep his commandments and do what
pleases him. And this is his commandment, that
we believe in the name of his Son Jesus Christ
and love one another, just as he commanded us.
Whoever keeps his commandments abides in
God, and God abides in him. And by this we
know that he abides in us, by the Spirit whom he
has given us. (1 John 3:22–24)

Everyone who believes that Jesus is the
Christ has been born of God, and everyone who
loves the Father loves whoever has been born of
him. By this we know that we love the children of
God, when we love God and obey his commandments. For this is the love of God, that we keep
his commandments. And his commandments are
not burdensome. (1 John 5:1–3)

Jesus said "If you keep my commandments, you will abide in my love, just as I have kept my Father's commandments and abide in his love. These things I have spoken to you, that my joy may be in you, and that your joy may be full." (John 15:10–11)

If anyone does sin, we have an advocate with the Father, Jesus Christ the righteous. He is the propitiation for our sins, and not for ours only but also for the sins of the whole world. And by this we have come to know him, if we keep his commandments. Whoever keeps his word, in him truly the love of God is perfected. By this we may know that we are in Jesus: whoever says he abides in him ought to walk in the same way in which Jesus walked. (1 John 2:1–5)

Jesus said "You are my friends if you do what I command you. No longer do I call you servants, for the servant does not know what his master is doing, but I have called you friends, for all that I have heard from my Father I have made known to you." (John 15:14–15)

While he (Jesus) was still speaking to the people, behold, his mother and his brothers stood outside, asking to speak to him. But he replied to the man who told him, "Who is my mother, and who are my brothers?" And stretching out his hand toward his disciples, he said, "Here are my mother and my brothers! For whoever does the will of my Father in heaven is my brother and sister and mother." (Matthew 12:46–50)

Although Jesus was a son, he learned obedience through what he suffered. And being made perfect, he became the source of eternal salvation to all who obey him. (Hebrews 5:8–9)

Jesus said "Everyone who comes to me and hears my words and *does them*, I will show you what he is like: he is like a man building a house, who dug deep and laid the foundation on the rock. And when a flood arose, the stream broke against that house and could not shake it, because it had been well built. But the one who hears God's words *and does not do them* is like a man who built a house on ground without a foundation. When the stream broke against it, immediately it fell, and the ruin of that house was great." (Luke 6:47–49)

Jesus said "Blessed are those who hear the word of God and keep it!" (Luke 11:28)

If what you heard in the beginning (God's word) abides in you, then you too will abide in the Son and in the Father. And this is the promise that he made to us—eternal life. (1 John 2:24–25)

Neither circumcision counts for anything nor uncircumcision, but keeping the commandments of God. (1 Corinthians 7:19)

Jesus said "Not everyone who says to me "Lord, Lord" will enter the kingdom of heaven, but the one who does the will of my Father who is in heaven." (Matthew 7:21)

The world is passing away along with all its desires, but whoever does the will of God abides forever. (1 John 2:17)

Did you know that *not following a commandment from* God was the first sin ever committed by humans, Adam and Eve? The sin of not following a commandment of God is what caused mankind to fall, creating the complete mess that mankind is in now, and why we needed Jesus to come and save us in the first place. God was personally with Adam and Eve, face-to-face in the Garden of Eden. Everything was perfect. God gave Adam this commandment, face-to-face.

> *And the Lord God commanded the man*, saying "Of every tree of the garden you may freely eat; but of the tree of the knowledge of good and evil you shall not eat, for in that day you eat of it you shall surely die." (Genesis 2)

> Now the serpent was more cunning than any beast of the field which the Lord God had made. And he said to the woman, "Has God indeed said 'You shall not eat of every tree of the garden'?" And Eve said to the serpent, "We may eat the fruit of the trees of the garden; but the fruit of the tree which is in the midst of the garden, God has said, 'You shall not eat it, nor shall you touch it, lest you die'." Then the serpent said to the woman, "You will not surely die. For God knows that in the day you eat of it your eyes will be opened, and you will be like God, knowing good and evil." (Genesis 3)

Eve ate the fruit and gave it to Adam, and he ate it also. This was God's response to Adam for doing this:

> *Because* you have heeded the voice of your wife, and have eaten from the tree which *I commanded you, saying, "You shall not eat of it"*: Cursed is the ground for your sake; In toil you shall eat of it all the days of your life. Both thorns and thistles it shall bring forth for you, and you shall eat of the herb of the field. In the sweat of your face you shall eat bread till you return to the ground, for out of the dust you were taken: for dust you are, and to dust you shall return. (Genesis 3:17–19)

Many, if not the majority, of the counseling clients in my Christian counseling practice are Christians. Frequently, they make the statement, "I love God, and I want to please him." But they do not know how to do this. "How do I love God?" They often ask. The numerous above Bible passages make it clear. God himself said over and over again in the Bible, "If you love me, you will do my commandments." How do you know what God's commandments are? Read the Bible regularly, and work toward doing what it says in your life. Trust me; you will be happy when you do. God tells his children all throughout the Bible the things he would like them to do. When we do them, this is how we love God, and it makes him happy. When we don't do what he says, we are sinning.

CHAPTER 3

The Good Things Jesus Does *for* Us if We Love and Follow Him

This chapter reveals God's statements in the Bible about what he will do *for* the people that love and follow him. We discussed earlier that one of the good things that God does for his people is he saves them from their sins. This chapter explains that process in more depth.

This first listed Bible passage explains how sin initially entered the world through one man, Adam. Sin was later removed from the world by one man, Jesus.

> Therefore, just as sin came into the world through one man (Adam), and death through sin, and so death spread to everyone because all sinned, Adam was a type of the one who was to come (Jesus).
>
> But the free gift is not like the trespass. For if many died through one man's trespass (Adam's), much more have the grace of God and the free gift by the grace of that one man Jesus Christ abound for many. And the free gift is not like the result of that one man's sin. For the judgment fol-

lowing one trespass brought condemnation, but the free gift following many trespasses brought justification. For if, because of one man's trespass (Adam's), death reigned through that one man, much more will those who receive the abundance of grace and the free gift of righteousness reign in life through the one man Jesus Christ.

Therefore, as one trespass led to condemnation for all men, so one act of righteousness led to justification and life for all men. For as by the one man's disobedience the many were made sinners, so by one man's obedience the many will be made righteous. Where sin increased, grace abounded all the more, so that, as sin reigned in death, grace also might reign through righteousness leading to eternal life through Jesus Christ our Lord. (Romans 5:12–21)

The New Testament explains in a variety of ways the benefits we get from Jesus taking on all of our sins and getting punished in our place. First, Jesus died with the world's sins taken off of each of us and placed on him, effectively removing our sins from us. Those that love and follow him get the benefit of this great sacrifice he made to save us.

You were all sinners. But you were washed, you were sanctified, you were justified in the name of the Lord Jesus Christ and by the Spirit of our God. (1 Corinthians 6:9–11)

Jesus himself bore our sins in his body on the tree, that we might die to sin and live to righteousness. By his wounds you have been healed. For you were straying like sheep, but have now returned to the Shepherd and the Overseer of your souls. (1 Peter 2:24–25)

You, who once were alienated and hostile in mind doing evil deeds, he has now reconciled in his body of flesh by his death, in order to present you holy and blameless and above reproach before him, if indeed you continue in the faith, stable and steadfast, not shifting from the gospel that you have heard. (Colossians 1:21–23)

An angel of the Lord appeared to Joseph saying, "Joseph, son of David, do not fear to take Mary as your wife, for that which is conceived in her is from the Holy Spirit. She will bear a son, and you shall call his name Jesus, for he will save his people from their sins." (Matthew 1:20–21)

And you, who were dead in your trespasses and the uncircumcision of your flesh, God made alive together with him, having forgiven us all our trespasses, by cancelling the record of debt that stood against us with its legal demands. This he set aside, nailing it to the cross. He disarmed the rulers and authorities and put them to open shame, by triumphing over them in him. (Colossians 2:13–15)

Christ redeemed us from the curse of the law by becoming a curse for us—for it is written, "Cursed is everyone who is hanged on a tree"—so that in Christ Jesus the blessing of Abraham might come to the Gentiles, so that we might receive the promised Spirit through faith. (Galatians 3:13–14)

God chose you as the firstfruits to be saved, through sanctification by the Spirit and belief in the truth. To this he called you through our gospel, so that you may obtain the glory of our Lord Jesus Christ. (2 Thessalonians 2:13–14)

Jesus has appeared once for all at the end of the ages to put away sin by the sacrifice of himself. And just as it is appointed for man to die once, and after that comes judgment, so Christ, having been offered once to bear the sins of many, will appear a second time, not to deal with sin but to save those who are eagerly waiting for him. (Hebrews 9:26–29)

We have been sanctified through the offering of the body of Jesus Christ once and for all. (Hebrews 10:10)

Grace to you and peace from God our Father and the Lord Jesus Christ, who gave himself for our sins to deliver us from the present evil age, according to the will of our God and Father, to whom be the glory forever and ever. (Galatians 1:3–5)

For freedom Christ has set us free; stand firm therefore, and do not submit again to the yoke of slavery. (Galatians 5:1)

All have sinned and fall short of the glory of God, and are justified by his grace as a gift, through the redemption that is in Christ Jesus, whom God put forward as a propitiation by his blood, to be received by faith. (Romans 3:23)

God shows his love for us in that while we were still sinners, Christ died for us. Since, therefore, we have now been justified by his blood, much more shall we be saved by him from the wrath of God. For if while we were enemies we were reconciled to God by the death of his Son, much more, now that we are reconciled, shall we be saved by his life. More than that, we also rejoice in God through our Lord Jesus Christ, through whom we have now received reconciliation. (Romans 5:8–11)

Jesus took our sins off of us, put them on himself, and got put to death with our sins on him in our place. This makes us completely sinless in the eyes of God: *if* we accept what he did for us, and if we follow him as our savior. A major benefit of this is now that we are sinless toward God, we are allowed to enter into eternal life in heaven when we die. This is what God tells us about our eternal life in the New Testament:

Jesus abolished death and brought life and immortality to light through the gospel. (2 Timothy 10)

Whoever receives Jesus' testimony sets his seal to this, that God is true. For he whom God has sent utters the words of God, for he gives the Spirit without measure. The Father loves the Son and has given all things into his hand. Whoever believes in the Son has eternal life. (John 3:33–36)

Jesus said "Whoever drinks of earthly water will be thirsty again, but whoever drinks of the water that I will give him will never be thirsty again. The water that I will give him will become in him a spring of water welling up to eternal life." (John 4:13–14)

Jesus said "Truly, truly, I say to you, whoever hears my word and believes him who sent me has eternal life. He does not come into judgment, but has passed from death to life." (John 5:24)

Jesus said "I am the living bread that came down from heaven. If anyone eats this bread, he will live forever. And the bread that I will give for the life of the world is my flesh." (John 6:51)

Jesus said "I am the light of the world. Whoever follows me will not walk in darkness, but will have the light of life." (John 8:12)

Jesus said "I came that they may have life and have it abundantly." (John 9:10)

I write these things to you who believe in the name of the Son of God that you may know that you have eternal life. (1 John 5:13)

Jesus said "Do not labor for the food that perishes, but for the food that endures to eternal life, which the Son of Man (Jesus) will give you. For on him God the Father has set his seal." (John 6:27)

Jesus said "My sheep hear my voice and I know them, and they follow me. I give them eternal life, and they will never perish, and no one will snatch them out of my hand. My Father, who has given them to me, is greater than all, and no one is able to snatch them out of the Father's hand. I and the Father are one." (John 10:27–30)

Jesus said "I am the way, and the truth, and the life. No one comes to the Father except through me. If you had known me, you would have known my Father also. From now on you do know him and you have seen him." (John 14:6–7)

For as in Adam all die, so also in Christ shall all be made alive. (1 Corinthians 22)

Eternal life in heaven. *Eternal.* A billion years is just a drop in the bucket compared to eternity. God made a way so that *anyone* who asks Jesus to be their Lord and savior and tries their best to follow him in their daily lives will be in a paradise beyond words forever. In paradise with him and the rest of their new, perfected family, which are all of the other people that chose to follow Jesus. An eternity in a paradise so amazingly wonderful. Heaven is so fantastic that Bible writers, such as John and Paul, who God brought to heaven and showed it to them, were unable to put it into words. It was so unbelievably great that when Paul returned, God had to put a horrible thorn in his side to bring him back to reality because his head was spinning from the awesomeness of it. Thank you, Jesus. Please sign me up. Eternity there with you in paradise.

In addition to removing our sins and giving us eternal life, Jesus does many other good things for those that follow him while they are still alive on earth. These are some of the additional benefits revealed to us in the New Testament:

Jesus preached to the people about the benefits they would get if they followed him. One of his most famous teachings on this is called the Beatitudes. Jesus said the following:

"Blessed are the poor in spirit, for theirs is the kingdom of heaven.

Blessed are those who mourn, for they shall be comforted.

Blessed are the meek, for they shall inherit the earth.

Blessed are those that hunger and thirst for righteousness, for they will be satisfied.

Blessed are the merciful, for they shall receive mercy.

Blessed are the pure in heart, for they shall see God.

Blessed are the peacemakers, for they shall be called sons of God.

Blessed are those who are persecuted for righteousness' sake, for theirs is the kingdom of heaven.

Blessed are you when others revile you and persecute you and utter all kinds of evil against you falsely on my account. Rejoice and be glad, for your reward is great in heaven, for so they persecuted the prophets who were before you." (Matthew 5:2–11)

The other good things Jesus does for us are as follows:

Jesus said "Do not be anxious saying, 'What shall we eat?' or 'What shall we wear?' Don't be worried. Your heavenly Father knows that you need them all. But seek first the kingdom of God and his righteousness, and all these things will be added to you." (Matthew 6:31–33)

Jesus said "Ask and it will be given to you; seek, and you will find; knock, and it will be opened to you. For everyone who asks receives, and the one who seeks finds, and to the one who knocks it will be opened. Or which one of you, if his son asks him for bread, will he give him a stone? Or if he asks for a fish, will give him a serpent? If you then, who are evil, know how to give good gifts to your children, how much more will your Father who is in heaven give good things to those who ask him?" (Matthew 7:7–11)

For the love of Christ controls us, because we have concluded this: that one has died for all, that those who live might no longer live for themselves but for him who for their sake died and was raised. (2 Corinthians 5:14–15)

For godly grief produces a repentance that leads to salvation without regret, whereas worldly grief produces death. (2 Corinthians 7:10)

For you know the grace of our Lord, Jesus Christ, that though he was rich, yet for your sake he became poor, so that you by his poverty might become rich. (2 Corinthians 8:9)

Whoever sows sparingly will reap sparingly, and whoever sows bountifully will also reap bountifully. (2 Corinthians 9:6)

Jesus said to the apostle Paul, "My grace is sufficient for you, for my power is made perfect in weakness." Therefore I will boast all the more gladly of my weaknesses, so that the power of Christ may rest upon me. For the sake of Christ, then, I am content with weaknesses, insults, hardships, persecutions, and calamities. For when I am weak, then I am strong. (2 Corinthians 12:9–10)

The Lord is faithful. He will establish you and guard you against the evil one. (2 Thessalonians 3:3)

Let us then with confidence draw near to the throne of grace, that we may receive mercy and find grace to help in time of need. (Hebrews 4:16)

For Christ has entered, not into holy places made with hands, which are copies of the true things, but into heaven itself, now to appear in the presence of God on our behalf. (Hebrews 9:24)

Do not neglect to show hospitality to strangers, for thereby some have entertained angels unaware. (Hebrews 12:2)

The Lord is my helper; I will not fear; what can man do to me? (Hebrews 13:6)

If any of you lacks wisdom, let him ask God who gives generously without reproach, and it will be given to him. But let him ask in faith, with no doubting. (James 1:5–6)

Blessed is the man who remains steadfast under trial, for when he has stood the test he will receive the crown of life, which God has promised to those who love him. (James 1:12)

Do not be deceived, my beloved brothers. Every good gift and every perfect gift is from above, coming down from the Father of lights with whom there is no variation or shadow due to change. (James 1:16)

Submit yourselves therefore to God. Resist the devil, and he will flee from you. Draw near to God, and he will draw near to you. Humble yourselves before the Lord, and he will exalt you. (James 4:7, 8, and 10)

God gave us a spirit not of fear but of power and love and self-control. (2 Timothy 1:7)

The Lord will give you understanding in everything. (2 Timothy 2:7)

Jesus said "Everyone who acknowledges me before men, I also will acknowledge before my father who is in heaven, but whoever denies me before men, I also will deny before my father who is in heaven." (Matthew 10:32–33)

Jesus said "Whoever receives you receives me, and whoever receives me receives him who sent me." (Matthew 10:40)

Jesus said "Come to me, all who labor and are heavy laden, and I will give you rest. Take my yoke upon you, and learn from me, for I am gentle and lowly in heart, and you will find rest for your souls. For my yoke is easy and my burden is light." (Matthew 11:28–30)

Jesus said "I desire mercy, and not sacrifice." (Matthew 12:7)

I want you to be free from anxieties. (1 Corinthians 7:32)

If anyone loves God, he is known by God. (1 Corinthians 8:3)

Jesus said "Again I say to you, if two of you agree on earth about anything they ask, it will be done for them by my Father in heaven. For where two or three are gathered in my name, there am I among them." (Matthew 18:19–20)

Jesus said "Truly, I say to you, if you have faith and do not doubt, even if you say to this mountain 'Be taken up and thrown into the sea' it will happen. And whatever you ask in prayer, you will receive, if you have faith." (Matthew 21:21–22)

Jesus said "Therefore I tell you, whatever you ask in prayer, believe that you have received it and it will be yours. And whenever you stand praying, forgive, if you have anything against anyone, so that your Father who is in heaven may forgive you your trespasses." (Mark 11:24–26)

Jesus said "Blessed are you when people hate you and when they exclude you and revile you and spurn your name as evil, on account of the Son of Man (Jesus)! Rejoice on that day, and leap for joy, for behold, your reward is great in heaven; for so their fathers did to the prophets." (Luke 6:22–23)

I Am sure of this, that he who began a good work in you will bring it to completion at the day of Jesus Christ. (Philippians 1:6)

Jesus said "And I tell you, everyone who acknowledges me before men, the Son of Man (Jesus) also will acknowledge before the angels of God, but the one who denies me before men will be denied before the angels of God." (Luke 12:8)

Jesus said "Stay dressed for action and keep your lamps burning, and be like men who are waiting for their master to come home from the wedding feast, so that they open the door to him when he comes and knocks. Blessed are those servants whom the master finds awake when he comes. Truly, I say to you, he will dress himself for service and have them recline at the table, and he will come and serve them." (Luke 12:35–37)

Jesus said, "Whoever believes in me, believes not in me but in him who sent me. And whoever sees me sees him who sent me. I have come into the world as light, so that whoever believes in me may not remain in darkness." (John 12:44–46)

The Lord is at hand; do not be anxious about anything, but in everything by prayer and supplication with thanksgiving let your requests be made known to God. And the peace of God, which surpasses all understanding, will guard your hearts and your minds in Christ Jesus. (Philippians 4:5–7)

What you have learned and received and heard and seen in me—practice these things, and the God of peace will be with you. (Philippians 4:9)

I have learned in whatever situation I am to be content. (Philippians 4:11)

God will supply every need of yours according to his riches in glory in Christ Jesus. (Philippians 4:19)

Jesus said "For the Father himself loves you, because you have loved me and have believed that I came from God." (John 16:27)

Jesus said "I have said these things to you, that in me you may have peace. In the world you may have tribulation. But take heart, I have overcome the world." (John 16:33)

Therefore, since we have been justified by faith, we have peace with God through our Lord Jesus Christ. Through him we have also obtained access by faith into this grace in which we stand, and rejoice, in hope of the glory of God. More than that, we rejoice in our sufferings, knowing that suffering produces endurance, and endurance produces character, and character produces hope, and hope does not put us to shame, because God's love has been poured into our hearts through the Holy Spirit who has been given to us. (Romans 5:1–5)

The God of peace will soon crush Satan under your feet. (Romans 16:20)

As you wait for the revealing of our Lord Jesus Christ, who will sustain you to the end, guiltless in the day of our Lord Jesus Christ. God is faithful, by whom you were called into the fellowship of his Son, Jesus Christ our Lord. (1 Corinthians 1:7–9)

No temptation has overtaken you that is not common to man. God is faithful, and he will not let you be tempted beyond your ability, but with the temptation he will also provide the way of escape, that you may be able to endure it. (1 Corinthians 10:13)

Now there are varieties of gifts, service and activities, but the same Spirit. It is the same God who empowers them all in everyone. To each is given the manifestation of the Spirit for the common good. For to one is given through the Spirit the utterance of wisdom, and to another the utterance of knowledge according to the same Spirit, to another faith by the same Spirit, to another gifts of healing by the one spirit, to another the working of miracles, to another prophecy, to another the ability to distinguish between spirits, to another various kinds of tongues, to another the interpretation of tongues. All these are empowered by one and the same Spirit, who apportions to each one individually as he wills. (1 Corinthians 12:4–11)

As you can see, there are *countless* good things that God does *for* those that love and follow him while we are still on earth and when we finally enter heaven.

CHAPTER 4

The Good Things Jesus Does *to* Us if We Love and Follow Him

T he next section contains New Testament Bible verses that explain the good things that God does *to* his followers. When we ask Jesus to save us, the Holy Spirit enters us and starts to transform us more and more to be like Jesus. This process begins the moment we get saved. Once we accept Jesus, and the more we learn God's word and live it out in our lives, the more God changes us to actually be like Jesus. This is an internal transformation while we are on earth, and it is only a small fraction of our transformation. When we die and enter heaven in the presence of God, we become completely transformed, body, soul, and spirit, into a heavenly being beyond earthly description. In the first part of this chapter, we will examine what the Bible says God does to his followers while they are still on earth. God informs us that when we are saved, he enters our body, while, at the same time, we enter into and become part of the body of Christ. This joining of our bodies with God's body happens partially while we are on earth, and it is completed and perfected when we get to heaven.

Whoever confesses Jesus is the Son of God, God
abides in him, and he in God. (1 John 4:15)

We know that the Son of God has come and has given us under-standing, so that we may know him who is true; *and we are in him who is true, in his Son Jesus Christ.* He is the true God and eternal life. (1 John 5:21)

There is therefore now no condemnation for those who are in Christ Jesus. (Romans 8:1)

Do you not know that you are God's tem-ple and that God's spirit dwells in you? If anyone destroys God's temple, God will destroy him. *For God's temple is holy, and you are that temple.* (1 Corinthians 3:16–17)

God raised the Lord (Jesus) and will also raise us up by his power. *Do you not know that your bodies are members of Christ? He who is joined to the Lord becomes one spirit with him.* (1 Corinthians 6:14–15 and 17)

Do you not know that your body is a temple of the Holy Spirit within you, whom you have from God? You are not your own, for you were bought with a price. So glorify God in your body. (1 Corinthians 6:19–20)
Now you are the body of Christ and individu-ally members of it. (1 Corinthians 12:27)

Examine yourselves, to see whether you are in the faith, Test yourselves. Or do you not realize this about yourselves, *that Jesus Christ is in you?* (2 Corinthians 13:5)

There is a mystery hidden for ages and gen-erations but now revealed to his saints. To them God chose to make known how great among the

Gentiles are the riches of the glory of this mystery, *which is Christ in you, the hope of glory.* (Colossians 1:26–27)

In Jesus the whole fullness of deity dwells bodily, and you have been filled in him, who is the head of all rule and authority. (Colossians 2:9–10)

No one ever hated his own flesh, but nourishes it and cherishes it, just as Christ does *the church, because we are all members of his body.* "Therefore a man shall leave his father and mother and hold fast to his wife, and the two shall become one flesh." This mystery is profound, and I am saying that it refers to Christ and the church. (Ephesians 5:29–32)

Jesus said "When the Spirit of truth comes, he will guide you into all the truth, for he will not speak on his own authority, but whatever he hears he will speak, and he will declare to you the things that are to come. He will glorify me, for he will take what is mine and declare it to you. All that the Father has is mine; therefore he will take what is mine and declare it to you." (John 16:13–15)

May the God of hope fill you with all joy and peace in believing, so that by the power of the Holy Spirit you may abound in hope. (Romans 15:13)

Now we have received not the spirit of the world, but the Spirit who is from God, that we might understand the things freely given to us by God. And we impart this in words not taught by human wisdom but taught by the Spirit, interpreting spiritual truths to those who are spiritual. (1 Corinthians 2:12–13)

> *Speaking the truth in love, we are to grow up in every way into him who is the head, into Christ,* from whom the whole body, joined and held together by every joint with which it is equipped, when each part is working properly, makes the body grow so that it builds itself up in love. (Ephesians 4:15–16)

> If then you have been raised with Christ, seek the things that are above, where Christ is, seated at the right hand of God. Set your minds on the things that are above, not on the things that are on earth. For you have died, and *your life is hidden with Christ in God. When Christ who is your life appears, then you will appear with him in glory.* (Colossians 3:1–4)

Many of the Christians that I speak to about God are vaguely aware at best that when they follow Christ, God lives in them, and they have become part of the body of Christ. Hopefully, the above Bible passages will make you aware of this great reality.

The good things God does *for* those who love and follow him are magnified exponentially when we die and go to heaven. We will be completely transformed into something unspeakably glorious. What we are now on earth is not what we will become in heaven. In the next Bible passage, God explains this. He said our body while on earth is a seed, and inside this seed is a soul. The soul that will blossom out of this seed when we die and arrive in heaven is nothing like the seed it came out of (our bodies) and is much greater than the seed. Think of an acorn from a mighty oak tree. The acorn is small. When it is planted and sprouts, it doesn't grow into a second small acorn identical to the first. Rather, when the acorn sprouts and grows to its full development, it is a mighty oak tree that is much more spectacular and nothing at all like the small acorn it sprouted from. When we die and go to heaven, our spiritual bodies will be much more magnificent and much different from our earthly bodies, the seed which contained unblossomed soul. This is how God explains it:

> But someone will ask, "How are the dead raised? With what kind of body do they come?" You foolish person! What you sow does not come to life unless it dies. And what you sow is not the body that is to be, but a bare kernel, perhaps of wheat or of some other grain. But God gives it a body as he has chosen, and to each kind of seed its own body. For not all flesh is the same, but there is one kind for humans, another for animals, another for birds, and another for fish. There are heavenly bodies and earthly bodies, but the glory of the heavenly is of one kind, and the glory of the earthly is of another.
>
> So it is with the resurrection of the dead. What is sown is perishable; what is raised is imperishable. It is sown in dishonor; it is raised in glory. It is sown in weakness; it is raised in power. It is sown a natural body; it is raised a spiritual body. If there is a natural body, there is also a spiritual body. Thus it is written, "The first man Adam became a living being, the last Adam (Jesus) became a life-giving spirit." But it is not the spiritual that is first but the natural, and then the spiritual. The first man was from the earth, a man of dust; the second man is from heaven. As was the man of dust, so also are those who are of the dust, and as is the man of heaven, so also are those who are of heaven. Just as we have born the image of the man of dust, we shall also bear the image of the man of heaven (Jesus).

I tell you this, brothers: flesh and blood cannot inherit the kingdom of God, nor does the perishable inherit the imperishable. Behold! I tell you a mystery. We shall not all sleep, but we shall all be changed, in a moment, in the twinkling of an eye, at the last trumpet. For the trumpet will sound, and the dead will be raised imperishable, and we shall be changed. For this perishable body must put on the imperishable, and this mortal body must put on immortality. When the perishable puts on the imperishable, and the mortal puts on immortality, then shall come to pass the saying that is written: "Death is swallowed up in victory. O death, where is your victory? O death, where is your sting?" (1 Corinthians 15:35–55)

The following are more New Testament Bible passages in which God talks about his followers being magnificently transformed when they arrive in heaven. Additionally, some of the passages state that when we get to heaven, we will be God's children, and we will be transformed into the image of God:

> And we know that *for those who love God,* all things work together for good, for those who are called according to his purpose. For those whom he foreknew he also *predestined to be conformed to the image of his Son, in order that he might be the firstborn of many brothers.* (Romans 8:28–30)

God's goal for those who love him is to continually make them more and more like Jesus throughout their lives on earth. When we get to heaven, we will actually be brothers and sisters of Jesus.

> *See what kind of love the Father has given to us, that we should be called children of God; and so we are. Beloved, we are God's children now,*

*and what we will be has not yet appeared; but we
know that when he appears we shall be like him,
because we shall see him as he is.* And everyone
who thus hopes in him purifies himself as he is
pure. (1 John 3:1–3)

A religious leader asked Jesus if a person is
married on earth, are they still married in heaven
after they die? Jesus said, "The sons of this age
marry and are given in marriage, but those who
are considered worthy to attain to that age and
to the resurrection from the dead neither marry
nor are given in marriage, for they cannot die
anymore, *because they are equal to angels and are
sons of God, being sons of the resurrection.*" (Luke
20:34–36)

Assuming that you have heard about Jesus
and were taught in him, as the truth is in Jesus,
to put off your old self, which belongs to your
former manner of life and is corrupt through
deceitful desires, and to be renewed in the spirit
of your minds, and to *put on the new self, created
after the likeness of God in true righteousness and
holiness.* (Ephesians 4:21–24)

*Do you not know that the saints will judge the
world? Do you not know that we are to judge angels?*
(1 Corinthians 6:2–3)

You have put off the old self with its prac-
tices and have put on the new self, which is being
renewed in knowledge *after the image of its cre-
ator.* (Colossians 3:9–10)

You are a chosen race, a royal priesthood, a holy nation, a people for God's own possession, that you may proclaim the excellencies of him who called you out of darkness into his marvelous light. (1 Peter 2:9)

Now the Lord is the Spirit, and where the Spirit of the Lord is, there is freedom. And we all, with unveiled face, beholding the glory of the Lord, are being transformed into the same image from one degree of glory to another. For this comes from the Lord who is the Spirit. (2 Corinthians 3:17–18)

Our citizenship is in heaven, and from it we await a Savior, the Lord Jesus Christ, who will transform our lowly body to be like his glorious body, by the power that enables him even to subject all things to himself. (Philippians 3:20–21)

As you come to Jesus, a living stone rejected by men but in the sight of God chosen and precious, *you yourselves like living stones are being built up as a spiritual house, to be a holy priesthood,* to offer spiritual sacrifices acceptable to God through Jesus Christ. (1 Peter 2:4–5)

Do you not know that all of us who have been baptized into Christ Jesus were baptized into his death? We were buried therefore with him by baptism into death, in order that, just as Christ was raised from the dead by the glory of the Father, we too might walk in newness of life.

For if we have been united with him in a death like his, we shall certainly be united with him in a resurrection like his. We know that our old self was crucified with him in order that the body of sin might be brought to nothing, so that we would no longer be enslaved to sin. For one who has died has been set free from sin. Now if we have died with Christ, we believe that we will also live with him. We know that Christ, being raised from the dead, will never die again; death no longer has dominion over him. For the death he died he died to sin, once for all, but the life he lives he lives to God. So you must also consider yourselves dead to sin and alive to God in Christ Jesus. (Romans 6:3–11)

If we have died with Jesus, we will also live with him; if we endure, we will also reign with him. (2 Timothy 2:11–12)

There is laid up for me the crown of righteousness, which the Lord, the righteous judge, will award to me on that day, and not only me but also to all who have loved his appearing. (2 Timothy 4:8)

When the perfect comes, the partial will pass away. For now we see in a mirror dimly, but then face to face. Now I know in part; then I shall know fully, even as I have been fully known. (1 Corinthians 13:10 and 12)

So we do not lose heart. Though our outer self is wasting away, our inner self is being renewed day by day. *For this light momentary affliction is preparing for us an eternal weight of glory beyond all comparison,* as we look not to the things that are seen but to the things that are unseen. For the things that are seen are transient, but the things that are unseen are eternal. (2 Corinthians 4:16–18)

In Christ Jesus you are all sons of God, through faith. For as many of you as were baptized into Christ have put on Christ. There is neither Jew not Greek, there is neither slave nor free, there is no male and female, for you are all one in Christ Jesus. (Galatians 3:26–28)

In the next subsection of Bible passages, God explains to us that those who love and follow him, when they die, will be placed into marvelous positions in heaven. We will be adopted children of God the Father and brothers and sisters of Jesus. We will have all of the privileges of being in God's family that a person on earth has with his earthly immediate family: God is our Father, Jesus is our brother, and we will live in God's home as his children and have access to all that an immediate family member has access to. Once we decide to follow Jesus while on earth and become saved by him, we also immediately become heirs to God's kingdom. When we die and get to heaven, we will receive our inheritance: God will give his kingdom to us. This is what God says about it in his own words:

Jesus is the mediator of a new covenant, so that *those who are called may receive the promised eternal inheritance,* since a death has occurred that redeems them from the transgressions committed under the first covenant. For where a will is involved, the death of the one who made it must be established. For a will takes effect only at death, since it is not in force as long as the one who made it is alive. (Hebrews 9:15–17)

If you are Christ's, then you are Abraham's offspring, heirs according to the promise. I mean that the heir, as long as he is a child, is no different from a slave, though he is the owner of everything, but he is under guardians and managers until the date set by his father. In the same way we also, when we were children, were enslaved to the elementary principals of the world. But when the fullness of time had come, God sent forth his Son, born of woman, born under the law, to redeem those who were under the law, *so that we might receive adoption as sons. And because you are sons, God has sent the Spirit of his Son into your hearts, crying "Abba! Father!" So that you are no longer a slave, but a son, and if a son, then an heir through God.* (Galatians 3:29 and 4:1-7)

Blessed be the God and Father of our Lord Jesus Christ, who has blessed us in Christ with every spiritual blessing in the heavenly places, even as he chose us in him before the foundation of the world, that we should be holy and blameless before him. *In love, he predestined us for adoption as sons through Jesus Christ,* according to the purpose of his will, to the praise of his glorious grace, with which he has blessed us in the Beloved. In him we have redemption through his blood, the forgiveness of our trespasses, according to the riches of his grace, which he lavished upon us, in all wisdom and insight making known to us the mystery of his will, according to his purpose, which he set forth in Christ as a plan for the fullness of time, to unite all things in him, things in heaven and things on earth.

In him we have obtained an inheritance, having been predestined according to the purpose of him who works all things according to the counsel of his will, so that we who were the first to hope in Christ might be to the praise of his glory. *In him you also, when you heard the word of truth, the gospel of your salvation, and believed in him, were sealed with the promised Holy Spirit, who is the guarantee of our inheritance until we acquire possession of it, to the praise of his glory.* (Ephesians 1:1–14)

Blessed be God the Father of our Lord Jesus Christ! According to his great mercy, he has caused us to be born again to a living hope through the resurrection of Jesus Christ from the dead, to an inheritance that is imperishable, undefiled, and unfading, kept in heaven for you, who by God's power are being guarded by faith for a salvation ready to be revealed in the last time. (1 Peter 1:2–7)

The outcome of your faith is the salvation of your souls. (1 Peter 1:9)

When the goodness and loving kindness of God our Savior appeared, he saved us, not because of works done by us in righteousness, but according to his own mercy, by the washing of regeneration and renewal of the Holy Spirit, whom he poured out on us richly through Jesus Christ our Savior, *so that being justified by his grace we might become heirs according to the hope of eternal life.* (Titus 3:4–7)

Jesus who sanctifies and those who are sanctified have one source. That is why he is not ashamed to call them brothers, saying "I will tell your name to my brothers; in the midst of the congregation I will sing your praise." "*Therefore Jesus had to be made like his brothers in every respect, so that he might become a merciful and faithful high priest in the service of God, to make propitiation for the sins of the people.* For because he himself has suffered when tempted, he is able to help those who are being tempted." (Hebrews 2:10–12 and 17)

Listen, my beloved brothers, has not God Chosen those who are poor in the world to be rich in faith and heirs of the kingdom, which he has promised to those who love him? (James 2:5)

Because I have heard of your faith in the Lord Jesus and your love toward all the saints, I do not cease to give thanks for you, remembering you in my prayers, that the God of our Lord Jesus Christ, the Father of glory, may give you a spirit of wisdom and of revelation in the knowledge of him, having the eyes of your hearts enlightened, *that you may know what is the hope to which he has called you, what are the riches of his glorious inheritance in the saints,* and what is the immeasurable greatness of his power toward us who believe, according to the working of his great might, that he worked in Christ when he raised him from the dead and seated him at his right hand in heavenly places. *And he put all things under his feet and gave him as head over all things to the church, which is his body, to the fullness of him who fills all in all.* (Ephesians 1:15–23)

Jesus said "The righteous will shine like the sun in the kingdom of their Father." (Matthew 13:43)

Jesus said "Fear not, little flock, for it is your Father's good pleasure to give you the kingdom." (Luke 12:32)

Jesus is preparing rooms in God's own house for those that love God. He will then personally come and take you to live with him in heaven.

> *Jesus said "Let not your hearts be troubled. Believe in God; believe also in me. In my father's house are many rooms. If it were not so, would I have told you that I go to prepare a place for you? And if I go and prepare a place for you, I will come again and take you to myself, that where I am you may be also. And you know the way to where I am going."* (John 14:1–4)

Home is a place you can either stay at or go back to if you wanted to. Earth is not our home. We cannot stay here, and once we leave, we can never come back. It is just a place we are temporarily passing through. Heaven will be our home.

> Those that have faith in God acknowledged that they were strangers and exiles on the earth. For people who speak thus make it clear that they are seeking a homeland. If they had been thinking of that land from which they had gone out, they would have had an opportunity to return. But as it is, they desire a better country, that is, a heavenly one. Therefore God is not ashamed to be called their God, for he has prepared for them a city. (Hebrews 11:13–16)

> God, being rich in mercy, because of the great love with which he loved us, even when we were dead in our trespasses, made us alive together with Christ—by grace you have been saved—and raised us up with him in the heavenly places in Christ Jesus, so that in the coming ages he might show the immeasurable riches of

his grace in kindness toward us in Christ Jesus.
For by grace you have been saved through faith.
And this is not of your own doing, it is a gift of
God. (Ephesians 2:4–7)

*What no eye has seen, nor ear heard, nor the
heart of man imagined, what God has prepared for
those who love him.* (1 Corinthians 2:9)

Now in Christ Jesus you who were once
far off have been brought near by the blood of
Christ. For he himself is our peace, who has made
us both one and has broken down in his flesh the
dividing wall of hostility by abolishing the law of
commandments expressed in ordinances, that he
might create in himself one new man in place of
the two, so making peace, and might reconcile
us both to God in one body through the cross,
thereby killing the hostility.
*For through Jesus we both have access in
one spirit to the Father. So then you are no longer
strangers and aliens, but you are fellow citizens with
the saints and members of the household of God,
built on the foundation of the apostles and prophets,
Christ Jesus himself being the cornerstone, in whom
the whole structure, being joined together, grows
into a holy temple in the Lord. In him you are also
being built together into a dwelling place for God by
the Spirit.* (Ephesians 2:13–22)

*This mystery is that the Gentiles are fellow
heirs, members of the same body, and partakers
of the promise in Christ Jesus through the gospel.*
(Ephesians 3:6)

God the Father has delivered us from the domain of darkness and transferred us to the kingdom of his beloved Son, in whom we have redemption, the forgiveness of sins. (Colossians 1:13–14)

God has not destined us for wrath, but to obtain salvation through our Lord Jesus Christ, who died for us so that whether we are awake or asleep we might live with him. (1 Thessalonians 5:9–10)

According to God's promise we are waiting for new heavens and a new earth in which righteousness dwells. (2 Peter 3:13)

At one time you were darkness, but now you are light in the Lord. Walk as children of light (for the fruit of light is found in all that is good and right and true), and try to discern what is pleasing to the Lord. (Ephesians 5:8–10)

Living in paradise forever. As the adopted children of God the Father and siblings of Jesus. In a resurrected body, something like the angels, which is infinitely more glorious than the one we are in now. We will have our own room in God's house that Jesus personally made for us, just as a child on earth has their own room in their parents' (family's) home. Members of God's immediate family. When we arrive in heaven, we will receive our inheritance, which is the kingdom of God. Reread this paragraph again and let it all sink in. Now do you see why I so strongly encourage all Christians to read the Bible? There is so much good in there that people are missing out on in their lives if they do not read it.

CHAPTER 5

The Good Things Jesus Does *through* Us for the Sake of Others if We Love and Follow Him

I t is *amazing* what God will do for those who love and follow him when they reach heaven. But once saved, God has a very important purpose for us while we are still alive on earth. As I stated earlier, God loves to do his good works through, and in cooperation with, his children on earth. You have to realize that the only way a person comes to Christ is if someone else tells him or her about Jesus. People are not born with an inherent knowledge about God. The reason why I am able to write this present book is because people have told me about God earlier in my life. Now that we are saved by Jesus and follow him, we have to tell other people about him so that they can do the same thing. Christians are God's children. He wants us to work in the family business while we are still on earth. There is a lot of good work that needs to be done, and God does much of it through us. The main things he wants his children to do on earth have to do with helping other people. He wants us to love them, help them, take care of them, tell them about him so they too can be saved, become members of his family, and receive all of the benefits of membership in God's family that we have. He also wants us to be disciples and make disciples out of other people. We are God's family members, human representations of Jesus on earth, and his personal ambassadors to the rest of the world. He has good work that he wants his children here to build his family that will be together in heaven one day. This is what God has to say about it:

> In Christ, God was reconciling the world to himself, not counting their trespasses against them, *and entrusting to us the message of reconciliation. Therefore, we are ambassadors for Christ, God making his appeal through us.* We implore you on behalf of Christ, to be reconciled to God. For our sake he made himself to be sin who knew no sin, so that in him we might become the righteousness of God. *Working together with Him, then, we appeal to you not to receive the grace of God in vain.* (2 Corinthians 5:19–21 and 6:1)

> *Jesus said "You are the salt of the earth. You are the light of the world. Let your light shine before others so that they may see your good works and give glory to your Father who is in heaven."* (Matthew 5:13–16)

> Jesus said, *"Go into all the world and proclaim the gospel to the whole creation. Whoever believes and is baptized will be saved, but whoever does not believe will be condemned."* (Mark 16:15–16)

> *After Jesus rose from the dead, he told his disciples "All authority in heaven and on earth has been given to me. Go therefore and make disciples of all nations, baptizing them in the name of the Father and of the Son and of the Holy Spirit, teaching them to observe all that I have commanded you. And*

behold, I am with you always, to the end of the age.
(Matthew 28:18–20)

Jesus said "If anyone serves me, he must follow
me; and where I am, there will my servant be also.
If anyone serves me, the Father will honor him."
(John 12:26)

The following Bible passages are specific instructions God gave
to his children concerning the work he would like us to do on earth
and some of the powers he will give us that will equip us to do his
work. Much of the work that God wants his children to do while still
on earth is this: love and care for other people.

Jesus told the people "I say to you, Love
your enemies and pray for those who persecute
you, so that you may be sons of your father who
is in heaven." (Matthew 5:44–45)

Jesus said "If you forgive others their trespasses, your heavenly Father will also forgive you,
but if you do not forgive others their trespasses,
neither will your father forgive your trespasses."
(Matthew 6:14–15)

Jesus said, "When you give a dinner at
a banquet, do not invite your friends or your
brothers or your relatives or your rich neigh-
bors, lest they also invite you in return and you
be repaid. But when you give a feast, invite the
poor, the crippled, the lame, the blind, and you
will be blessed, because they cannot repay you.
For you will be repaid at the resurrection of the
just." (Luke 14:12–14)

Jesus said "A new commandment I give to you, that you love one another: just as I have loved you, you are to love one another. By this all people will know that you are my disciples, if you have one for one another." (John 13:34–35)

Jesus said "Judge not, and you will not be judged; condemn not, and you will not be condemned; forgive, and you will be forgiven; give, and it will be given to you. Good measure, pressed down, shaken together, running over, will be put into your lap. For with the measure you use it will be measured back to you." (Luke 6:37–38)

This commandment we have from God: whoever loves God must also love his brother. (1 John 4:21)

Jesus said "This is my commandment, that you love one another as I have loved you." (John 15:12)

Beloved, if God so loved us, we also ought to love one another. No one has ever seen God; if we love one another, God abides in us and is perfected in us. (1 John 4:11)

We who are strong have an obligation to bear with the failings of the weak, and not to please ourselves. Let each of us please his neighbor for his good, to build him up. For Christ did not please himself, but as it is written, "The reproaches of those who reproached you fell on me." (Romans 15:1–3)

> God is love, and whoever abides in love abides in God, and God abides in him. By this is love perfected with us, so that we may have confidence in the day of judgment. (1 John 4:16–17)

> Beloved, let us love one another, for Love is from God, and whoever loves has been born of God and knows God. (1 John 4:7)

> For you were called to freedom, brothers. Only do not use your freedom as an opportunity for the flesh, but through love serve one another. For the whole law is fulfilled in one word: "You shall love your neighbor as yourself." (Galatians 5:13–14)

The above Bible passages make it very clear: one of God's main wishes for his children on earth is that we love others.

Other works that God wants his children to do in this world are as follows:

> Do nothing from rivalry or conceit, but in humility count others as more significant than yourselves. Let each of you look not only to his own interests, but also to the interests of others. (Philippians 2:3–4)

> Is anyone among you suffering? Let him pray. Is anyone among you sick? Let him call for the elders of the church, and let them pray over him, anointing him with oil in the name of the Lord. And the prayer of faith will save the one who is sick, and the Lord will raise him up. And if he has committed sins, he will be forgiven. Therefore, confess your sins to one another and pray for one another, that you may be healed.

The prayer of the righteous person has great power as it is working. (James 3:13–16)

For to me to live is Christ, and to die is gain. If I am to live in the flesh, that means fruitful labor for me. Yet which I shall choose I cannot tell. I am hard pressed between the two. My desire is to depart and be with Christ, for that is far better. But to remain in the flesh is more necessary on your account. (Philippians 1:21–24)

My brothers, if anyone among you wanders from the truth and someone brings him back, let him know that whoever brings back a sinner from his wandering will save his soul from death and will cover a multitude of sins. (James 5:19–20)

The fruit of the Spirit (Holy Spirit) is love, joy, peace, patience, kindness, goodness, faithfulness, gentleness, self-control; there is no law against such things. And those who belong to Christ Jesus have crucified the flesh with its passions and desires. If we live by the Spirit, let us walk by the Spirit. Let us not become conceited, provoking one another, envying one another. (Galatians 5:22–26)

Please understand this; the following Bible passages explain that whatever works God calls you to do, he will equip and empower you to do it.

Blessed be the God and Father of our Lord Jesus Christ, the Father of mercies and God of all comfort, who comforts us in all our affliction, so that we may be able to comfort those who are in any affliction, with the comfort with which we ourselves are comforted by God. For as we share abundantly in Christ's sufferings, so through Christ we share abundantly in comfort too. If we are afflicted, it is for your comfort and salvation; and if we are comforted, it is for your comfort, which you experience when you patiently endure the same sufferings that we suffer. Our hope for you is unshaken, for we know that as you share in our sufferings, you will also share in our comfort. (2 Corinthians 1:3–7)

Such is the confidence that we have through Christ toward God. Not that we are sufficient in ourselves to claim anything as coming from us, but our sufficiency is from God, who has made us competent to be ministers of a new covenant. (2 Corinthians 3:4–6)

Seventy-two followers of Jesus returned to Him with joy, saying, "Lord, even the demons are subject to us in your name!" And Jesus said to them, "I saw Satan fall like lightening from heaven. Behold, I have given you authority to tread on serpents and scorpions, *and over all the power of the enemy,* and nothing shall hurt you. Nevertheless, do not rejoice in this, that the spirits are subject to you, but rejoice that your names are written in heaven." (Luke 10:17–20)

Be strong in the Lord and in the strength of his might. Put on the whole armor of God, that you may be able to stand against the schemes of the devil. For we do not wrestle against flesh and blood, but against the rulers, against the authorities, against the cosmic powers over this present darkness, against the spiritual forces of evil in the heavenly places. Therefore, take up the whole armor of God, that you may be able to withstand in the evil day, and having done all, to stand firm. (Ephesians 6:10–13)

Jesus said, "If you had faith like a grain of mustard seed, you could say to this mulberry tree, 'Be uprooted and planted in the sea,' and it would obey you." (Luke 17:6)

For what we proclaim is not ourselves, but Jesus Christ as Lord, with ourselves as your servants for Jesus' sake. For God, who said, "Let light shine out of darkness," has shone in our hearts to give the light of the knowledge of the glory of God in the face of Jesus Christ. (2 Corinthians 4:5–6)

Therefore, be imitators of God, as beloved children. And walk in love, as Christ loved us and gave himself up for us, a fragrant offering and sacrifice to God. (Ephesians 5:1–2)

Therefore, my beloved brothers, be steadfast, immovable, always abounding in the work of the Lord, knowing that in the Lord your labor is not in vain. (1 Corinthians 15:58)

Jesus said "Truly, truly, I say to you, whoever believes in me will also do the works that I do; and greater works than these will he do, because I am going to the Father. Whatever you ask in my name, this I will do, that the Father may be glorified in the Son. If you ask anything in my name, I will do it." (John 14:12–13)

And God is able to make all grace abound to you, so that having sufficiency in all things at all times, you may abound in every good work. (2 Corinthians 9:8)

Finally, brothers, rejoice. Aim for restoration, comfort one another, live in peace; and the God of love and peace will be with you. (2 Corinthians 13:11)

I have been crucified with Christ. It is no longer I who live, but Christ who lives in me. And the life I now live in the flesh I live by faith in the Son of God, who loved me and gave himself for me. (Galatians 2:20)

The one who sows to the Spirit (Holy Spirit) will from the Spirit reap eternal life. And let us not grow weary of doing good, for in due season we will reap, if we do not give up. So then, as we have opportunity, let us do good to everyone, and especially to those who are of the household of faith. (Galatians 6:8–10)

We are God's workmanship, created in Christ Jesus for good works, which God prepared beforehand, that we should walk in them. (Ephesians 2:10)

For it is God who works in you, both to will and to work for his good pleasure. Do all things without grumbling or questioning, that you may be blameless and innocent, children of God without blemish in the midst of a crooked and twisted generation, among whom you shine as lights in the world, holding fast to the word of life. (Philippians 2:13–16)

Whatever you do, work heartily, as for the Lord and not for men, knowing that from the Lord you will receive the inheritance as your reward. You are serving the Lord Christ. (Colossians 3:23–24)

For we know, brothers loved by God, that he has chosen you, because our gospel came to you not only in word, but also in power and in the Holy Spirit and with full conviction. (1 Thessalonians 1:4–5)

If anyone cleanses himself from what is dishonorable, he will be a vessel for honorable use, set apart as holy, useful to the master of the house, ready for every good work. (2 Timothy 2:21)

As each has received a gift, use it to serve one another, as good stewards of God's varied grace. (1 Peter 4:18)

Conclusion

The following passage is Jesus's last prayer to his Father right before he went to the garden of Gethsemane to wait to be apprehended by the Roman soldiers and to be crucified for our sake. The prayer is all about how much he loves us. We were the last thing on his mind as he was about to be taken and crucified. I highlighted the last part in bold type, because this part of Jesus's prayer is specifically to the Father for *us*. Right after this, he went to be crucified. In Jesus's words:

> Jesus said "Father, the hour has come; glorify your Son that the Son may glorify you, since you have given him authority over all flesh, to give eternal life to all whom you have given him. And this is eternal life, that they know you the only true God, and Jesus Christ whom you have sent. I glorified you on earth, having accomplished the work that you gave me to do. And now, Father, glorify me in your own presence with the glory that I had with you before the world existed.
>
> I have manifested your name to the people whom you gave me out of the world. Yours they were, and you gave them to me, and they have kept your word. Now they know that everything that you have given me is from you. For I have given them the words that you gave me, and they have received them and have come to know in truth that I came from you; and they have believed that

you sent me. I am praying for them. I am not praying for the world but for those whom you have given me, for they are yours. All mine are yours, and yours are mine, and I am glorified in them. And I am no longer in the world, but they are in the world, and I am coming to you. Holy Father, keep them in your name, which you have given me, that they may be one, even as we are one. While I was with them, I kept them in your name, which you have given me. I have guarded them, and not one of them have been lost except the son of destruction, that the scripture might be fulfilled. But now I am coming to you, and these things I speak in the world, that they may have my joy fulfilled in themselves. I have given them your word, and the world has hated them because they are not of the world, Just as I am not of the world. I do not ask that you take them out of the world, but that you keep them from the evil one. They are not of the world, just as I am not of the world. Sanctify them in the truth; your word is truth. As you sent me into the world, so I have sent them into the world. And for their sake I consecrate myself, that they also may be sanctified in truth.

I do not ask for these only, but also for those who will believe in me through their word (us!) that they may all be one, just as you, Father, are in me and I in you, that they may also be in us, so that the world may believe that you have sent me. The glory that you have given me I have given to them, that they may be one even as we are one, I in them and you in me, that they may become perfectly one, so that the world may know that you sent me and loved them even as you loved me. Father, I

desire that they also, whom you have given me, may be with me where I am, to see my glory that you have given me because you loved me before the foundation of the world. O righteous Father, even though the world does not know you, I know you and these know that you have sent me. I made known to them your name, and I will continue to make it known, that the love with which you have loved me may be in them and I in them." (John 17:1–26)

If there was any doubt that Jesus loves us, Jesus's last prayer to his Father should put it to rest for you.

In summary, this book is a compilation of all of the good things God said he would do for those that love and follow him. It is easy to be one of these people. To get all of God's promises, do the following:

1. Tell Jesus you accept him as your God and savior. Agree to turn your life over to his will and follow him.
2. Read the Bible consistently. Start in the New Testament, and read one or two pages a day. But do it every day. When you finish the New Testament, then start reading the Old Testament. And *do* what God says to do in your lives, the best you can. Remember, God says that the way to love him is to know what he says and to do it.
3. Talk with him daily as you would a loving father. This is prayer.
4. Attend a Bible-based church when you can.
5. Reap the benefits of God's great promises to his children in this life and the next.

In closing, this is one of Jesus's last statements to the world, found on the last page of the Bible, in the Book of Revelation:

Jesus said "Behold, I am coming soon, bringing my recompense with me, to repay everyone for what he has done. I am the Alpha and the Omega, the first and the last, the beginning and the end." (Revelation 22:12)

Are You Praying to God for Help or Guidance and not Hearing from Him?

While reading through various books in the Bible, I realized that three of Jesus's parables are connected. They give us information on how to get an understanding of God and receive his guidance that many of us may be missing out on. Below are the three parables and explanations of how they are connected and how we can access God's wisdom and understanding in our daily lives.

In Matthew 24:1–51 and 25:1–13, Jesus was informing the people about his second coming at the rapture of his people. He went on to further describe his second coming in the rapture in Matthew 25:14–30 in a parable called "The Parable of the Talents."

The Parable of the Talents

Jesus was talking to the people about his second coming: "For it will be like a man going on a journey, who called *his servants and entrusted them to his property.* (Followers of Jesus are his servants—us). To one he gave five talents (a talent is a very large sum of money, equivalent to approximately a year's salary); to another, two; and to another, one, *each according to his ability. Then he went away.* He who had received the five talents went at once and traded with them, and made five talents more. So also he who had two talents made two talents more. But he who had received the one talent went and dug in the ground and hid his master's money. Now after a long time the master of those servants came and settled accounts with them. And he who had received the five talents came forward, bringing five talents more, saying, "Master, you have delivered me five talents; here I have made five talents more." His master said to him, "Well done, good and faithful servant. You have been faithful over a little; I will set you over much. Enter into the joy of your master." And he also who had the two talents came forward, saying, "Master, you delivered me two talents; here I have made two talents more." His master said to him, "Well done, good and faithful servant. You have been faithful over a little; I will set you over much. Enter into the joy of your master." He who had received the one talent came forward, saying, "Master, I knew you to be a hard man, *reaping where you did not sow, and gathering where you scattered no seed,* so I was afraid, and I went and hid your talent in the ground. Here you have what is yours." But the master answered him, "You wicked and slothful servant! You knew that *I reap where I have not sown and gather where I scattered no seed?* Then you ought to have invested my money with the bankers, and *at my coming* I should have received what was my own with interest. So take the talent from him and give it to him who has ten talents. *For to everyone who has more will be given, and he will still have an abundance. But from the one who has not, even what he has will be taken away.* And cast the worthless servant into the outer darkness. In that place there will be weeping and gnashing of teeth."

The Parable of the Sower

I n Mark, Chapter 4, Jesus gave two other parables that are connected to the Parable of the Talents. The three parables appear to be talking about the same thing. When they are connected, you get the full meaning of Jesus's message, and it is profound. This is the Parable of the Sower:

> Jesus was speaking to the people and he said, "Listen! A sower went out to sow. And as he sowed, some seed fell along the path, and the birds came and devoured it. Other seed fell on the rocky ground, where it did not have much soil, and immediately it sprang up, since it had no depth of soil. And when the sun rose, it was scorched, and since it had no root, it withered away. Other seed fell among the thorns, and the thorns grew up and choked it, and it yielded no grain, and other seeds fell into good soil and produced grain, growing up and increasing and yielding thirtyfold and sixtyfold and a hundredfold." (Mark 4:3–8)

> Those with Jesus asked him to explain the meaning of this parable to them, and he did. Jesus said, "The sower sows the *word (the word of God, which is the Bible)*. And these (people) are along the path where the word is sown: when they hear, Satan immediately comes and takes

away the word that is sown to them. And these (people) are the ones sown on the rocky ground: the ones who, when they hear the *word*, immediately receive it with joy. And they have no root in themselves, but endure for a while; then, when tribulation or persecution arises on account of the word, immediately they fall away. And others (people) are the ones sown among thorns. There are those who hear the *word*, but the cares of the world and the deceitfulness of riches and the desires for other things enter in and choke the word, and it proves unfruitful. But those (people) that were sown on the good soil are those who *hear the word and accept it and bear fruit, thirtyfold and sixtyfold and a hundredfold."* (Mark 4:14–20)

The Parable of a Lamp under a Basket

I n the next sentence, Jesus gives the parable of A Lamp Under a Basket in Mark 4:21–25. Jesus said, "Is a lamp brought in to be put under a basket, or under a bed, and not on a stand? For nothing is hidden except to be made manifest; nor is anything secret except to come to light. If anyone has ears to hear, let him hear. *Pay attention to what you hear:* (Jesus is talking about hearing the word of God—the Bible and what it teaches): *with the measure you use* (*using* what the God tells us in the Bible—the next two sentences are exactly the same as in the Parable of the Talents) *it will be measured to you, and still more will be added to you. For the one who has, more will be given, and the one who has not, even what he has will be taken away."*

What is the point of all of this? The Parable of the Talents, the Parable of the Sower, and the Parable of the Lamp Under a Basket all make the same statements. "To everyone who has, more will be given to you. But the one who has not, even what he has will be taken away." Therefore, I believe they are talking about the same thing. In the Parable of the Talents, the master (God) called his servants and entrusted them his property. Those who believe in and follow God are his servants, which are us. He entrusted them his property—he gave them each varying amounts of talents, which is something valuable; each talent in money terms is a year's salary. Then he went away. He eventually came back and wanted to know what his servants did with the talents that were given to them. Well, we follow God. We are his servants. But he didn't give us a great deal of money and go away. Therefore, he must be talking about something else.

In the Parable of the Sower, Jesus explains clearly that he is talking about the word of God. He sows the word of God in us—we have the Bible which contains all of God's word for us. For some people, it is fruitful, for others it is not. Immediately after explaining that the Parable of the Sower means God giving us the word of God, in the next sentence Jesus gives the Parable of a Lamp Under a Basket and is still talking about the word of God. He makes this all-important statement, which is the same statement he used in the Parable of the Talents: *"Pay attention to what you hear (hear the word of God—read the Bible): with the measure you use(know what the Bible says and use it, or do what it says to do) it will be measured to you, and still more will be added to you. For the one who has, more will be given, and from the one who has not, even what he has will be taken away.'*

What does this mean? We who claim to know and follow God must first *know his word (read the Bible)*. Beyond this, we must *use it or do what it says*. The more we actually do what the Bible says, the more God will reveal himself to us and give us himself in an overflowing abundance. If we don't know his word and/or do not do it, he will take understanding of him that he made available to us away. So if you are going through troubles in your life and are praying to God for help but are not hearing anything from him, this may help: *Are you reading the Bible and actually doing what it says to do in your life?* If not, you might not be getting all of the help and guidance from God that you can. It is as if he is saying, "You aren't using what I *already provided for you in my word that I gave you, yet you want me to give you more? If you use what I already gave you, I will be happy to give you more, and I will give you abundantly more. If you ignore what I already gave you in my word, even that I will take away your understanding of it because you don't want it."* If you aren't reading the Bible, you need to start and *do what it says*. Additionally, since the Parable of the Talents was to help inform us about his second coming, it sounds like when he does return, he will gather all of us and make us give an account of *how we managed his property that was entrusted to us—how much did we use or do the word of God that he gave us.*

About the Author

Michael Kotch is a licensed psychologist, receiving his doctorate degree in clinical psychology from Widener University in 2003. He has been practicing at an outpatient Christian counseling agency since 2006. He has worked in a variety of counseling and human services agencies since 1989, and he has taught psychology at the undergraduate level. Michael has been the fifth and sixth grade religious instruction teacher at his local church from 2012 to the present. He has been an avid daily Bible reader since he gave his life to Jesus in 1999. He has read multiple versions of the Bible, from cover to cover, over eight times, and he has read the entire Jewish Tanakh. He feels called to teach others the Bible and to encourage everyone to read it and live it out in their daily lives. Michael has two additional books scheduled for release in the fall of 2018:

Lessons for Christians from the Trials of Job (Christian Faith Publishing)

Faith Through Hardships Draws Others to Christ (West Bow Press)

Michael lives in a small town in Southeast Pennsylvania with his wife, Mary; his son, Jacob; and his daughter, Johanna.

CPSIA information can be obtained
at www.ICGtesting.com
Printed in the USA
BVHW071522271118
534133BV00002B/90/P